The Xenophobe's® Guide to The Greeks

Alexandra Fiada

Oval Books

Published by Oval Books
335 Kennington Road
London SE11 4QE
United Kingdom

Telephone: +44 (0)20 7582 7123
Fax: +44 (0)20 7582 1022
E-mail: info@ovalbooks.com
Web site: www.ovalbooks.com

First published by Ravette Publishing, 1994
Reprinted/updated: 1997, 1998

First published by Oval Books, 2000
Reprinted 2001
New edition 2003

Editor – Catriona Tulloch Scott
Series Editor – Anne Tauté

Cover designer – Jim Wire, Quantum
Printer – Cox & Wyman Ltd
Producer – Oval Projects Ltd

Xenophobe's® is a Registered Trademark.

To Charles Haldeman who so
loved and appreciated the Greeks.

With thanks to Manuela Berki
for her invaluable help.

ISBN: 1-903096-32-4

Contents

The Greek population is 11 million, compared with 3 million Albanians; 2 million mixed peoples composed of Bulgarians, Greeks, Albanians, Serbs, Turks and gypsies in Fyrom (Former Yugoslav Republic of Macedonia); 8 million Bulgarians, and 70 million Turks.

Nationalism and Identity

Forewarned

'Xenos' in Greek means both the stranger and the guest. Even before the time of Homer, hospitality in Greece had not only become a kind of ritual with religious overtones, but had also developed into an art form. The Greeks were the first 'xenophiles' in the world – that is, they liked any friendly stranger.

At the other end of the scale, 'xenophobe' in Greek means the native who doesn't like the strangers who visit his land. In English, the term is more generic and generally applies to the traveller who fears the strangers he encounters. (To a Greek this is a bit odd, for if he is afraid of strangers, why did he ever leave home?)

But he did and he does. It is necessary, therefore, to allay the fears of xenophobe travellers, who, had they any say in the matter, would prefer to enjoy the beauties of foreign lands without having to encounter their inhabitants. Since this is an unavoidable evil, the first thing to realise is the importance of winning the natives over, which is fairly easy once you know what makes them tick. To this end, take heed. When in Greece avoid looking down your nose at anything Greek because it will get you nowhere. The Greeks have famously long noses to look down.

How They See Themselves

The Greeks are the personification of contradiction and nowhere is this more pronounced than in the way they see themselves. A Greek, speaking to other Greeks about the Greeks, more often than not will be outspokenly critical, even downright rude about how fellow Greeks conduct themselves in any given situation. His pronouncements will be received by his cronies with much head-nodding, appropriate expletives of acquiescence and, further, with even more disparaging remarks. However, woe betide any hapless foreigner who may suggest that the Greeks, as a race, are not the 'salt of the earth'. The same Greeks, who a minute ago were so disparaging of themselves, will turn on him – like a tigress defending her cub – and, while extolling Greek virtues, accuse him of any sins of omission or commission his country has committed against Greece since the dawn of civilization – and beyond.

It is not that the Greeks do not acknowledge their shortcomings; it is rather that they do not recognise any outsider having the right to point them out. "When we were building the Parthenon," they might well declare, "you were painting yourselves blue."

Modern Greeks pat themselves on the back because, although they fall short of what their ancestors achieved, they managed to come through a 400-year Turkish occupation (one of the cruellest in history) with their identity, their religion, their customs and their language virtually intact.

However, this occupation prevented them from enjoying the benefits of the Renaissance (for which they provided the means) and precluded their taking part in the Age of Exploration, the Enlightenment, and the Social and Industrial Revolutions. When they threw off the Turkish yoke in 1827 they found themselves living in a country that had lost more than three quarters of its former territory. Pitched headlong into the industrial age without the education and funds to cope with it, they have been trying to catch up with the West ever since.

The transition was traumatic for Greek psyche. They not only feel a sense of inadequacy compared with ancient and Byzantine Greeks because they have failed to recreate the 'Great Greece' of their forefathers, but they carry a burden of resentment towards the West. It's a state of mind continually fanned by what the Western world has achieved by exploiting the Greek heritage, which makes the Greeks feel as if they have been robbed of it. The result is a bizarre inferiority-cum-superiority complex vis à vis the West. 'We gave them the light of knowledge and we have been left with the light from cheap tallow candles' is one of their favourite sayings.

On the other hand, nothing shakes their fundamental belief that they are the most intelligent and the most ingenious people on earth, and also the most brave.

To quote Greek writer, Nikos Demou: 'The modern Greek, when he looks in the mirror, sees himself either as Alexander the Great or as Kolocotronis [the greatest general of the Greek War of Independence] or, at least, as Aristotle Onassis. Never as Karaghioz [the figure of popular shadow theatre – a sort of Caliban, but minus the malice]. Yet, in reality, he is Karaghioz who dreams that he is Alexander the Great. Karaghioz of many trades, of many faces, who is perpetually hungry and who is master of only one art: play acting.'

How Others See Them

'We are all Greeks,' declared Shelley. 'Our laws, our literature, our religion, our arts have their roots in Greece.' Yet, until recently, slang dictionaries defined a 'Greek' as 'a gambler; a card-sharp; a cheat; a highwayman' – probably because so many of the refugees who fled to the European capitals after Constantinople fell to the Turks had to live on their wits to survive.

The Greeks' dual personality has fascinated historians and travellers for centuries. Some saw them through rose-coloured spectacles, some through dark, distorted lenses, others did not see them at all, but wrote as if they did. The laurel however goes to an American, Judge N. Kelly, who managed to contain all their contradictions in a nutshell:

'In the tribunal of relentless history, the Greek has always been proven to be less than equal to circumstances, although from the point of intellect he has always had supremacy.

'The Greek is most intelligent, but also conceited; active, but also disorganised; with a sense of honour, but also full of prejudices; hot-headed, impatient, but also a fighter. [...] One moment he fights for the truth and the next he hates the man who refuses to serve a lie.

'A strange creature, untameable, inquisitive, half-good, half-bad, fickle, of uncertain mood, self-centred, foolish-wise – the Greek. Pity him, admire him, if you wish: classify him, if you can.'

Special Relationship

A Greek-American used to hand out visiting cards that stated in bold letters: 'I'd rather do business with a thousand Turks than with one Greek.' On the reverse was the name of his business, in handsome copperplate: *Mike's Funeral Parlor.*

The word 'Turk' alone raises the hackles of even the most cosmopolitan of Greeks, though what they really detest is Turkey as a concept and not individual Turks. Their reasons are understandable: they have had a surfeit of Turkish treatment since the mass slaughter of Greeks at the fall of Constantinople in 1453.

Throughout the resulting occupation, bands of white-kilted resistance fighters from the Greek highlands staged revolt after unsuccessful revolt. In 1821 they were lucky: they liberated part of Greece, but at a heavy price. 'Better an hour's free life,' ran the revolutionary anthem, 'than 40 years in bondage.' Their slogan, 'Freedom or Death', still rings in Greek ears and their martial songs blare from every radio on emotion charged anniversaries.

In a second round of warfare with the Turks, the

Greeks liberated Epirus, Macedonia and West Thrace, but, after ten victorious years, their campaign in Turkey ended in 1922 in a complete disaster. In more recent years the Turkish occupation of almost half of the island of Cyprus added considerable fuel to the embers of the ancient fire, with the result that whenever the question of solving the Cyprus problem is raised at the United Nations, vociferous demonstrators march down the streets of the Greek cities in support of the Greek-Cypriots.

Modern Greeks not only behave as if the events of those years happened yesterday, they also blame the Turkish occupation for all the faults in their character.

How They See Others

Apart from the Turks, the Greeks do not harbour any ill-feelings towards any other nationality. Certainly they do not particularly like the Bulgars and the Slavs north of their borders who, not content with Greek territories already gained, have expressed the intention to extend their borders south to the Aegean.

Nor are they over-fond of the Albanians, who, having managed to capitalise on the Greek Civil War, dragged the region of North Epirus behind the Iron Curtain with half a million Greeks in it. Yet Fate takes unexpected turns, and now these former aggressors are flooding Greece as economic refugees – and the Greeks are busy trying to keep them out.

As for other nations, the Greeks have a collective word *coutófragi* (meaning 'stupid Franks') which encompasses the whole Western world. In all probability the word is a remnant of the 13th-century occupation of Greece by the Franks of the Fourth Crusade – a real clash of civilizations since the uncouth, iron-clad knights crashed into the highly sophisticated Byzantine Empire, smashing wantonly whatever they did not understand.

Of later date are various generalities: the Turks are *boudaládes* – that is, fat and stupid; or *ápisti*, meaning 'infidels'; the Slavs, the Bulgarians in particular, are *gourounomítes*, that is, 'pig-nosed', or *kommitadzídes*, after the especially murderous bandits who were roaming Macedonia at the turn of the century, trying to coerce the Greek population (then living under Turkish rule) to turn Bulgar. These days, Bulgarian women are doing a great deal towards establishing more cordial relations with the Greeks. After the fall of the Communist regime, they too came over the border (along with assorted Rumanians, Ukranians, Russians and Georgians) to ply the world's most ancient profession among the affluent Greek peasants. Their impact is such that wives are demanding the government takes preventive measures, while provincial bars and cabarets post signs proclaiming: 'Tonight: Fresh Bulgarian Women'.

Having been part of the European Union and the Eurozone for several years now, the Greeks avoid calling their fellow-members names, but old generalities still endure: the Italians are considered to be *macaronádes* – 'spaghetti-eaters', meaning good-for-nothings (the Greeks have not forgotten that they soundly beat the Italian army in the Second World War). The French are known for their elegance and culture, but they are also seen as 'gigolos' or 'cocottes', depending on the gender, or 'cunning diplomats' (which is not meant as a compliment); the Germans are workaholics; the Irish are alcoholics; the Scots are stingy, the English are the embodiment of punctuality, but emotionally cold ('cold-arsed' is the word used by the Greeks); and the Spanish are passionate lovers.

Outside Europe, the Latin Americans are either footballers or sexy samba dancers or cocaine barons; the whole of Africa is peopled by lazybones; the Egyptians are illiterate 'fellahs'; the Jews are stingy, but fantastic bargainers; and the Arabs are all Bedouins who would steal your fingers if you offered to shake hands.

The Americans are 'cowboys' who try to rule the world as if it were the Wild West. The Russians are *hahóli*, meaning clumsy mountains of flesh; the Chinese are as inscrutable as their language (the Greeks obviously do not say "It's all Greek to me". They say "It's all Chinese"). The rest of the world may go hang.

Surprisingly, the Greeks do not use other nations as the butt of their jokes. They keep the sport in the family, so to speak, reviling each other from province to province, from village to village and from island to island. The Cretans dislike the Peloponnesians, the Macedonians the Rumeliotes, the Epirotes the Thessalians, the islanders the mainlanders, the Athenians all the rest, and so on – until every rock and every hamlet is covered.

The international jokes which question the intelligence of one people or another are directed towards the Greeks from Pontos (the refugees from the cities on the Black Sea). For example:

Q: Why did the prostitute from Pontos who had been in the business for twenty years commit suicide?

A: Because she found out that all the other prostitutes were getting paid for it.

Or, an announcement at the airport:

'The Pontiots are requested not to spread corn on the runway. The big bird will come down without it.'

Greek gypsies are another popular subject because of their penchant for pilfering, their peddling, their innumerable children and their unspeakable dirt.

"Wife," asks the gypsy, seeing in the rear-view mirror that one of his countless brats has fallen off the back of his Datsun pick-up truck, "shall we stop to pick him up, or shall I get you with a new one?"

11

Character

The character of the Greeks, even at the time of Homer, could best be described as schizophrenic.

Neither education, upbringing nor wealth maketh the Man in Greece; nor does their lack produce the Knave. From the highest to the lowest walks of life, you may encounter both Alexander the Great (noble, brave, sincere, warmhearted, intelligent, broadminded, generous) and Caliban (mean, cunning, selfish, garrulous, conceited, slothful, envious and greedy) – often in the same person.

Individuality is the chief feature that characterises the Greeks, which precludes any attempt to box and label them as a people. After that comes their temperament which flourishes uninhibited throughout their waking hours. This is probably why the ancient sages saw fit to carve their maxims 'Nothing in excess' and 'Know thyself' on the portals of the Delphic Oracle in an attempt to persuade their fellow Greeks to curb their emotions. They were not heeded then any more than they are now. From Achilles (whose wrath caused so much unnecessary slaughter under the walls of Troy) to 19th-century Admiral Miaoulis (who torched the Greek fleet simply because he was at odds with the government), the Greeks give full vent to their emotions and damn the consequences.

Individualism

As the Greek joke goes: 'Why is the best business enterprise in Greece a kiosk? Because only one person can fit inside.' The Greeks nurture an outsize ego, which precludes any collective enterprise (unless a national disaster stares them in the face, whereupon they band together in a rare display of domestic unity). They also exhibit an outsized passion for freedom of choice – which has turned law circumvention into an art and has rendered them incapable of comprehending words like 'discipline', 'co-ordination' or 'system'.

'I' is the Greeks' favourite word. When a Greek poses the rhetorical question "Do you know who I am?", he clearly considers himself the centre of the world. He feels as if all the Greek heroes, sages and statesmen of old are ranging themselves behind him and therefore he expects you to pay homage to him (and to them). As an old man from Delphi explained, it is all very simple: "The Earth is the centre of the Universe; Greece is the heart of the Earth; Delphi is the centre of Greece and the Earth's navel; I am head man of Delphi, therefore I am the centre of the Universe."

Extreme Emotion

Self-control – although invented by the ancient Spartans – is not only unknown but also incomprehensible to the modern Greeks. They are eager in everything: their joys, their sorrows have no moderation. Enthusiasm comes much too easily to them. They shout, they yell, they rant and rave about important and unimportant issues alike, in happiness and in sorrow. No emotion is considered private enough to remain unexpressed and their excitement knows no bounds.

Their exuberance is often translated into a burning need to express themselves in some physical form. All over the world, people dance when they are happy. The Greeks are also liable to get up and dance away the deepest anguish from their heart, in a rhythm so solemn and heart-rending it makes expressionist ballet seem joyous by comparison.

"I have a devil inside me," explains Zorba the Greek in the homonymous novel by Kazantzakis. "Every time my heart is at the point of bursting, he tells me 'Dance!' and I dance. And my anguish goes away."

13

Indifference

On the other side of this red-hot coin of emotion lies the ice of indifference towards anything that has to do with public life. The phrase: 'Forget it, brother! I'm not going to stick my neck out in order to save the Roman nation' is quite common and denotes the supreme unwillingness of the majority of Greeks to show an active interest in anything that lies outside their immediate circle or will not benefit them personally.

Yet their schizoid nature also leads them to stage violent demonstrations or organize strikes – ruinous to the country's economy – at the drop of a hat. Whenever a particular union of workers feels its privileges are being threatened by some governmental decree or other, it cloaks its demands in high-faluting oratory, and its members, brimming with democratic ideals, march vociferously down the main streets of Athens. Traffic is brought to a standstill for hours, yet little is achieved other than a marvellous letting off of steam.

Strikes are, of course, a way of coercing the government to grant more privileges to this or that group of workers, but the peculiar thing in Greece is that they are invariably organized to coincide with the days preceding, or following, a weekend or a bank holiday.

Insecurity

According to an international survey, the Greek has the highest insecurity factor in the world. He is afraid to see himself as he really is, he dreads taking responsibility for his actions – and so he is unable to laugh at himself. Barricaded behind a façade of solemnity, he seeks to cover up his inadequacies, his self-doubts, his insecurity at all costs. He dreads the possibility of being taken lightly, of being considered not serious enough, and the more qualities he lacks, the graver and more pompous he appears. Two thirds of Greek society, haunted by the thought 'What will others say?', bury their spontaneity under layers of ill-fitting decorum.

Long Memories

The effort to sustain their identity through adversity has bequeathed to the Greeks a characteristic quite peculiar in modern times, which could be called 'historical time-lessness', or an overdeveloped sense of history.

Allusions to events and personages of the past – no matter how remote or obscure – crop up in everyday talk, newspaper editorials, radio and television commentaries, popular shows, song lyrics, and so forth. In coffee-houses or sitting rooms, conversations on current events invari-ably bring up comparisons with much older ones, with the result that political decisions of the past century are thrashed out or battles re-fought with a vehemence and attention to detail (actual or rumoured) that one would generally only expect from history professors.

The Greeks still call themselves 'Romans' (in colloquial Greek) which just goes to show how long their memories are. They remind you that the Byzantine Eastern Roman Empire was the only descendant of the earlier Roman one and lasted for a thousand years after its Western half had disintegrated – a distinction that of course makes them look down on the rest of Europe. No sooner had the Greeks joined the European Union than they suggested to the European Parliament that Greek be adopted for all deliberations.

The fact that history permeates Greek thinking to such an extent does not prevent the Greeks from being a very modern people, and at the same time helps them resist the uniformity of globalization. Yet this overdeveloped sense of history has a darker side: it prevents the Greeks from either forgetting or forgiving past slights or injuries.

For instance, the anti-American feelings that prevail today do not stem from current world politics or any real antagonism towards the United States, but because the U.S. supported the military Junta (who imposed a seven-year dictatorship in Greece) back in 1967, and then turned a blind eye when the Turks invaded Cyprus in 1974. From then on, the Greeks have blamed the U.S. for anything unpleasant that may happen to them – even bad weather.

Attitudes and Values

High Spirits

Despite their history and their nature, the Greeks enjoy life to the full. Their basic aim in life is to have a good time, to live comfortably here and now, and let the Devil take tomorrow. An exuberant folk-song to which villagers perform a skipping, stamping dance, has the refrain, 'This earth, upon which we are stepping, is going to receive us all.' A Greek may squander a month's salary for a feast and then spend the rest of the month without a penny in his pocket but with a gratified smile on his face. Greeks manage to have fun even under conditions that would plunge other people into the deepest gloom. Their unshakable optimism is well summarised in the common phrase 'God will provide', an expression which is more literally translated into 'God has', to which some wag is sure to retort: 'He has indeed, but He doesn't give it to us'.

A popular story has it that at the time of the Turkish occupation, a Greek made a bet with a Turkish cadi (judge) that in a year's time he would teach his donkey to read and write. He would then win a thousand gold coins, or lose his head if the donkey remained illiterate. The Greek borrowed a huge amount of money on his expectations, married a lovely girl, and spent his days feasting. "Aren't you going to do anything about the donkey?" asked a friend.

"Bah," said he. "By next year, either the donkey or the cadi will die. They are old..."

If I Were a Rich Man

The modern Greek's dearest dream is to make lots of money easily (preferably without lifting a finger), but it would never occur to him to hoard his wealth. "After all," he says, "shrouds have no pockets." He wants to have money in order to spend it as ostentatiously as possible – eating out, expensive cars, flashy (genuine) jewellery, designer clothes, fur coats, a house in the country and basketfuls of flowers to throw to the performers at the nightspots he patronises. All the rest – a successful career, a good marriage, a family – come second.

An old Cretan, raising his glass to toast the company, epitomised this dream by saying: "To our future enjoyment, pals. May we be abducted by beautiful girls – rich and short-lived."

Philótimo

Above all others, *philótimo* is the value the Greeks hold most dear. It refers to self-esteem and love of honour, respect for one's self and for others, a sense of fair play and duty. Usually, an appeal to it can make a Greek rise above the circumstances. A slight to the *philótimo*, though, is akin to the oriental loss of face: a serious offence, calling for satisfaction.

17

Behaviour

You Never Throw Grandma From the Train

The strength of Greek family ties is such that it is not uncommon to see three generations, or even four, sharing the same flat or (more usually) living within shouting distance of each other.

Despite Greek 'machismo', eight times out of ten the wife and mother (*Mamá* in Greek) is head of the family in all but name, particularly in the cities. Picturesque photos of women shouldering firewood and walking docilely behind their husband riding his donkey might lead you to think their lives are little better than that of women in Islamic countries. The well-veiled truth is that the majority of Greek men live under the cat's paw – but they would die rather than admit it. Even middle-aged bachelors, well established in their own flats, return almost daily to *Mamá* for a well-cooked meal and crisply ironed shirts.

For a Greek male, mother's cooking is always the best, and this is why, in his search for a wife, he is likely to choose someone of the same ilk. After all, a Greek saying maintains that 'the wife always takes after the mother-in-law'. Greek females train all their lives to become redoubtable mothers-in-law.

There is a traditional respect for the elderly in a family and, even if they no longer rule the roost as they did in older times, they are treated with affection and their desires humoured by their children. This may not be totally unrelated to the fact that they bring with them their state or union pensions (some quite substantial), but even when this is not the case, these same children had everything handed to them on a plate until they were well into adulthood, so now feel genuinely obliged to care for their parents in their old age. Besides, what would the neighbours say if they didn't? They would be talked about as people with no '*philótimo*' whatsoever.

King Herod Wouldn't Have Stood a Chance

Steer clear of Greek children. They may have angelic or cute urchin faces, but they are nearly all overfed, boisterous little menaces who are able to turn a room upside down faster than any demolition gang. Their parents may scream at them (preferably when everyone else is enjoying the sweetest of sleeps), but they spoil them rotten, giving in to even their most outrageous demands.

The result is that the majority of them develop all the worst Greek characteristics and none of the good ones. Fortunately, peer competition, higher education, the army and the harsh facts of life once they join the workforce usually kick them into shape and they acquire qualities one would not have thought them capable of.

Boys, being more pampered, are infinitely worse than girls. They will carry the family name – so nothing is too good for them, not to mention the old wives' tale that any refusal at a tender age will make the future man impotent. There is plenty of spanking and boxing of ears, and even empty threats ("I'll skin you alive"), but real discipline is rare. Every so often schoolchildren stage sit-ins against ministerial decrees requiring more education and less free time (with deleterious effect on the classrooms), while their parents look on complacently.

The Greeks adore their children and will provide unstintingly for them until such time as they find a good steady job, or until they marry. Relations with parents are very rarely severed, no matter what, nor do they decline to the polite acquaintance level, so common elsewhere.

Minor Matters

The Greeks are one of the very few non-racist people in the world. They will tell you racial jokes, but only because they cannot resist a good punchline – not because they subscribe to the sentiments behind it.

The ancient Greeks used to say that 'Whoever is not a Greek is a barbarian', but as Isocrates, orator of the 3rd century B.C., pointed out, 'Greeks we call those who share with us a common culture.' The modern Greek still feels the same. However, the modern Greek is also a schizophrene. More than a million foreigners (over 10% of the population) live and work in Greece – one third of them without work permits – including exchange students, political and economic refugees and tourists who came for a fortnight and are still there ten years later. Boatloads of destitute immigrants, packed like sardines, land regularly at outlying Greek islands, defeating the efforts of coastguards to turn them back. Once on Greek soil though they are succoured and given shelter by the local authorities.

The majority of Greeks do not distinguish between ethnic or religious groups of any kind, rather the reverse; they will go out of their way to make those who are 'different' feel more at home. However, this does not mean that the bouncer doing the 'face control' at the door of a fashionable nightspot is going to let you in if he thinks you can't afford it or if you smell of trouble. Greeks have a tendency to discriminate against those who lack the outward trappings of a 'civilized' person. If you do not look like a hard-core bum, or a chain-saw murderer, they will make you welcome even if your colour is bright green. But if you look like one of Ali Baba's Forty Thieves, no matter how decent you are, the Greeks will treat you like one – and ask questions afterwards.

A Dog's Life

The Greeks cannot be called animal lovers, although elderly spinsters who spend their meagre income on a houseful of stray cats or dogs are not that uncommon. As a rule, pets are one of the trappings of the upper classes and of those who try to ape them.

It wouldn't occur to any other pet owners to let a cat or a dog sleep on their bed or allow it the run of the house. In urban centres the fear of rabies (no cases of which have been reported for several decades) still moves over-protective mothers to warn their children not to go near 'the filthy dog'. Most people reserve their love for those animals that are useful to them, and for a canary or a goldfinch in a cage.

Manners

By misinterpreting the word 'freedom' the Greeks often confuse good manners with the servile behaviour they had to assume in order to survive under the Turkish yoke. As a result they believe that manifestations of politeness are only fit for slaves.

If you add to this their total lack of discipline (for which they are trained from a tender age), their wish to cut their betters down to size, and the general propensity to lower the standards (since it is always easier to go down than up), it is not surprising that manners are not one of the Greeks' strong points.

In Greece there is no class system with rigidly defined boundaries. The various classes, such as they are, mix casually, so bad manners can be encountered in the most unexpected places. Birth and a 'good' school are not prerogatives to any position and the concept of 'social upstart' or 'vulgar mushroom' has no equivalent.

Titles of nobility being prohibited by the Constitution, what the Greeks call the 'upper classes' are the nouveaux riches of today, coupled with the nouveaux riches of yesterday, a glittering dough which is leavened with a sprinkling of intellectuals, scientists, artists, top executives and politicians.

A few representatives of real old families (those whose lineage goes back to the Byzantine court, the Venetian *Libro d'Oro* and the powerful landowners and chieftains of the past) grace this social cake, rather in the manner of decorative cherries. But the majority of the old families have sunk, financially-speaking, to the middle of the cake. They may be numerous but not so many as to make a significant impact on the mannerless multitude.

Manners in Greece, therefore, are best described as cursory. Handshakes are only for introductions; friends say *"Yia sou"* (your health) and usually kiss on both cheeks – irrespective of sex or age. (Bowing and hand-kissing are reserved for priests and godfathers.)

In conversation though, it is considered intrusive to ask too many questions of a person's life and doings, even among friends. If a simple "How are you?" is met with a non-committal answer instead of a flood of details, you are not supposed to press the matter, however innocent the subject.

Proper queueing is almost unknown. People move (and drive) in an aggressive way and their acts are unadorned by any degree of consideration towards the welfare and peace of mind of their neighbours. Don't expect too many pleases and thank yous, or anything approaching punctuality, and don't expect a Greek to keep calm in a crisis. The one who does may (if lucky) live to regret it.

At the Table

Greek eating habits leave a lot to be desired.

Elbows go everywhere, even into side dishes, or flap shoulder high during the act of food cutting; fingers are not excluded from the dishes, nor is bone gnawing prohibited – even at expensive restaurants. Communal plates of appetizers or salads are quite common and dipping bits of bread into them to sop up the sauce and eat with the fingers is an accepted practice. A lot of people manage to chew their food while keeping their mouths wide open, and even more speak with their mouths full.

What the Greeks lack in table manners, though, they more than make up for in high spirits and conviviality. With a few Greeks around the table even the most formal dinner is bound to ring with laughter after the second course – to the benefit of all present.

Obsessions

The pursuit of easy money is one of the nation's chief obsessions, as indicated by the half-dozen state-controlled lotteries that create a couple of millionaires every week (and provide the Treasury with a tidy sum). Most Greeks buy their lottery tickets as a matter of course every week, the way other people buy a newspaper, and then devote their day-dreaming hours to planning what they will do with the money. The day of the draw (and its consequent disappointment) over, they renew their tickets with unabated optimism. In exactly the same way, when a decent return can be expected, anyone who has a feather to fly with will play the stock markets.

Greece may be a poor country, but in the 21st century the majority of Greeks have more money than they know how to spend. Money nurtures the ego of the nouvelle bourgeoisie and is manifested by their cars, furs and possessions. Their need to show off is understandable: most urban Greeks left their villages for the big cities (and for the capital in particular) only 50 to 60 years ago, so their urban mentality is not yet fully developed and they need at least two more generations in order to become true middle class.

The immense popularity of soap operas – *Dynasty*, *The Bold and the Beautiful* and their Brasilian and Greek imitations – is commensurate with the Greeks' insecurity. Through these they may live all the things they cannot afford or do not dare to do in real life. Equally popular are game shows, which, by offering the participants prizes from toasters to cars, or even better, hard cash, cater to their thirst for easy profit.

One might have expected the Greeks of all people to be obsessed with their classical heritage, but they are not. They may have long memories but they are nonchalant about this – clearly a case of familiarity breeding contempt. They remember their illustrious ancestors only when their glory can serve some practical purpose, such as naming a new company, or hosting the 2004 Olympic Games.

What they revere most are the heroes of the War of Independence. They are also fiercely proud of the fact that during the Second World War they fought against the Axis powers when the rest of Europe had capitulated: 'We can no longer say that the Greeks fight like heroes, we have to say that heroes fight like the Greeks,' said Winston Churchill.

Greek national holidays (25th March and 28th October) commemorate these two wars with much flag waving and emotion. The Greeks may be unconcerned about classical Greece, but should anyone impugn the least part of Greek ancestral lore, the modern Greeks rise to a man to its defence since they take any slight to their historical past as a personal affront, as a wound to their own *philótimo*.

Leisure and Pleasure

To the Englishman his home is his castle. To the Greek it is more like a wayside inn. He uses it (with rare exceptions) for practical purposes only – to rest, to change clothes, to have an occasional meal; he doesn't really live in it. What a Greek enjoys most is to go 'out'. Anywhere is preferable to staying in and, were he able to afford it, he would spend all his free time 'out', with his family and friends.

Those who stay 'in' out of choice, and whose outings are few and well chosen, are regarded as being somewhat eccentric – not to say downright misanthropic.

The average Greek is a very sociable being: he loves crowds; he wants to see and to be seen. No other country can boast of so many and such varied coffee houses, cafés, cafeterias, tavernas, restaurants, bars, nightclubs and *bouzouki* joints – all of which are absolutely packed, seven days a week.

Eating out is a Greek's favourite entertainment, particularly if the restaurant of his choice is also providing a live show or a musical accompaniment to the clinking of cutlery and glass. A Greek's idea of how best to spend his evening is to be with a *paréa*, that is, two or three couples from his vast collection of friends (their offspring included if no member of their families can be bullied into babysitting), merrily established at a taverna table (set in the open air from late spring to late autumn). There he proceeds to eat (excessively), to drink (in moderation) and to talk inanities (volubly) until late into the night, while his children maul the ever-present stray cats or fall asleep on their chairs.

This way of living is not peculiar to metropolitan life. There is no village in Greece, however humble, that does not boast the inevitable coffee houses and a couple of nightspots. There is no square throughout the country that on sunny days is not filled with tables and chairs on which most of the population of the area lounges as if there is no tomorrow.

A Greek needs at least four straight-legged chairs in order to lounge properly: sitting on one, he places each foot on the rungs of two more, directly in front of him; then, tilting back the chair he is sitting upon, he supports himself by draping one arm across the back of another chair, strategically placed at his side. He may even need a fifth chair, on which to park his jacket. (Modern cafés, by using untiltable chairs, have rather spoiled this ancient sport.)

Observing this, you might wonder who works and when. Rumour has it that only some 5% of the Greeks really work. The other 95% avoid it if they can.

Time Out

For the average Greek, work is something he does (cursing his luck) between holidays. There are some 12 official holidays in Greece, plus 22 working days of paid summer leave. These combined with the weekends, sick leaves and various strikes, enable an enterprising Greek to spend approximately one half of the year doing what he enjoys most: nothing. The result is that during the fortnight around the Christmas and Easter holidays and the two hottest summer months (July and August) the country almost comes to a standstill.

For short holidays – weekends and such – the Greek packs his wife, kids and mother-in-law into his car and heads for the countryside with the determination of a migrating lemming. Once there, he turns the young loose, then he sits once more at a taverna table. On Sunday night, the family joins the third of the Greek population that crawls back to the hapless capital through just three bottlenecks that pass for highways.

For longer holidays and for vacations, the obvious choice for those who live in the cities is to touch base, so to speak – that is, to return to their village of origin.

26

Middle-class Greeks also holiday abroad a good deal, mostly in organised groups. Shopping at department stores (upon which they descend like a swarm of locusts) is their first priority – sightseeing comes a definite second. Anything bought abroad is thought of as being of better quality, particularly if it is a bargain, and London sales are a great favourite. In fact, the slang word *'megla'* is a corruption of the phrase 'Made in England' and is used to denote elegance and supreme quality. By contrast, the word *'jampa'*, derived from 'Made in Japan', means very cheap.

Sex

According to a recent survey among well-travelled naughty girls ('good girls go to heaven – bad girls go everywhere'), the laurels of the 'Latin lover' grace the curly heads of the Greeks – to the great frustration of the Italians who come a (panting) second.

It is a well-known fact that female tourists from colder European regions flock every summer to the Greek islands with only one thing in mind: sex. There they meet with like-minded young men – the notorious *kamákia* (loosely translated as 'harpoons', because they 'hook' the girls) – who the rest of the year are ordinary, usefully employed, working men or students, but who, come summer, go on a sexual binge. They regard their amorous efforts as a service to humanity – giving the inhibited, pale, northern damsels a heady taste of sun-drenched virility and of tangy, velvet nights by the sea.

The Greeks are a very sensual people. Although there appears to be a middle-class restraint towards sex in general, nothing could be more misleading, because in fact their conservatism is only skin deep. Small wonder, when they are raised on the most adulterous mythology ever compiled, instead of innocuous nursery rhymes.

27

Were you to eavesdrop on an explicit conversation among a group of friends (whether the group is all male, all female, or mixed), you would scarcely believe your ears. The descriptions of what they did, how they did it, how many times and with whom (most Greek men and women are of the type who 'kiss and tell' – in the strictest confidence, of course) are so blatant and embellished with such graphic details that they would make the unexpurgated version of Aristophanes' plays seem tame by comparison.

Most men, whether happily married or not, consider themselves honour bound to cast out lures to any presentable female. The ensuing affair – as casual as it may be brief – rarely has repercussions on the marital status of either partner. The Greek male has affairs in order to nurture his ego and to add spice to his life and, no matter what he may say to the contrary, very seldom can he be coerced into divorcing his wife to marry his mistress. His wife – secure on her throne as queen bee of the family hive – will just shrug off the affair (if she hears about it), saying: "Poor darling, he can't say 'no' even to a female cat. He's a man; how can he go against nature?"

The wife is not averse to paying him back with the same coin. Yet usually the more unfaithful the wife is, the more her husband believes in her. "Cuckold your husband and don't resort to spells and philtres!" advises the old adage for achieving marital bliss.

The Greeks, despite their sensuality, or perhaps because of it, seem to have no need of the sexual aids so much in demand elsewhere. There are few sex shops in Greece and porno movies are watched more for the fun of it than as an inducement to a sexual act.

On the other hand, the Greeks have great faith in the aphrodisiac qualities of oysters and of olive oil, while they believe that fizzy drinks and soda water are quite detrimental to their virility.

For the Greeks, sex is God's gift to humanity and they

enjoy it for its own sake. (So much so that Greece has one of the highest abortion rates in Europe.) Should you try to explain to a Greek the precept of the western churches that making love for other than procreation purposes is a sin, he will laugh and say that, if God had such an intention, He would have made man and woman come on heat once a year, like the animals.

As the Greeks themselves say, 'Scratch a Greek and you will find a pagan'. The concept of 'sin' has very superficial roots in everyday Greek life. So, at least in the cities, there is no such thing as 'living in sin' with someone and, since by law women do not take the husband's name anymore (children can take the name of either parent), there is no way of knowing whether a couple is married or not. The words 'husband' and 'wife' are used indiscriminately, regardless of actual marital status.

Eating and Drinking

This is the land where ambrosia and nectar were invented, but so, of course, was hemlock. In true Greek style, there are many subtle and exquisite dishes, but there is also some commercial fare which although it will not kill you, tastes as if it might.

The ordinary Greek national dish is *phassoláda*, a thick bean-tomato-and-carrot soup (a meal in itself, particularly when supplemented by a smoked herring), while on Sundays and festive occasions roast baby lamb or kid, with potatoes baked in its gravy, is first choice.

Though each region has its own specialities (succulent dishes of meat cooked with various nuts and dried fruit, pies with original fillings among layers of wafer-thin homemade pastry, and colourful stuffed vegetables), the general tendency for an everyday meal is to make casseroles or stews.

Most food is cooked with translucent, pale gold-green olive oil or oil-derived margarine, which with the addition of ripe tomatoes, makes it swim in a bright scarlet sauce, ready to be eagerly scooped up with pieces of bread. 'White' dishes are flavoured with the tang of fresh lemons or finished with a creamy egg-and-lemon sauce.

Freshly slaughtered very young animals – veal, lamb, kid, suckling pig, spring chicken – are the Greeks' choice of 'good' meat. The silver and gold of Mediterranean fish – sea bream, dentex, gilt-head bream, sea bass, red mullet, sardine, whitebait and many others – form the basis of many delicately flavoured dishes, quite different from their Atlantic cold water cousins, smaller and tastier. Crustaceans, cephalopods and shellfish – fried, grilled or raw – make mouth-watering appetizers or even main dishes.

Vegetables – all kinds of fresh beans, aubergines, okra, courgettes, artichokes, potatoes, peppers, beetroot, broccoli, etc. – are cooked as main dishes (whether as part of a meat casserole or by themselves) and rarely eaten as garnishes.

The Greeks have a sweet tooth, so the variety of sweets and pastries they produce is endless. They make sweet preserves and jams from all fruits (including rose petals, orange blossoms, water-melon rinds and baby aubergines); they bake hundreds of traditional Greek breads, cakes and biscuits, and they copy all the Western confections and all the sinful, syrupy Middle-Eastern concoctions of crisp filo pastry, chopped nuts and spices.

Mealtimes are as erratic as the Greeks themselves: lunch is between 1.30 and 5.30 p.m. (depending on the individual's working hours) and dinner is after 10 p.m. Afternoon tea is non-existent, although a cup of coffee after the siesta hours is the universal reviver.

Though most Greeks declare scornfully, 'I never eat breakfast' (as if breakfast were a degenerate, almost depraved, habit), they usually have a coffee with a couple of rusks or biscuits around 7.30 in the morning, before setting out. At 11 a.m., being in urgent need of further sustenance they have a *tyrópitta* (a filo pastry oozing hot *féta* cheese).

Around noon, those who can afford the time meet friends for an apéritif (*ouzo* or beer) and a *poikilía* (a hot or cold appetizer) which can be a full meal in itself.

Everyday lunch or dinner is a simple affair: one dish – say, aubergines with minced veal and tomatoes, or pork with celery or chicken with okra – plus a tomato or lettuce salad. Cheese, especially crumbly white *féta* made of goat's or sheep's milk, is eaten during the meal and not at the end of it, and forkfuls of food alternate with pieces of bread dipped in the meat juices or in the salad dressing.

Delicious, sun-ripened fruits, so abundant in Greece, are the usual dessert and a hearty meal is always rounded off with Greek coffee. This is served black, in tiny cups, in one of numerous variations concerning the proportion of coffee and sugar to water. Greeks would not think it a proper cup of coffee unless it has a creamy brown foam on top and a quarter of an inch of muddy residue at the bottom. Aficionados drink it scalding hot, in small sips – the first followed by a profound sigh of satisfaction.

Meeting with friends, by chance or by design, usually calls for a drink (or several) at any time of the day or the night (there are no licensing hours in Greece), but it is very rare for a Greek to drink alone. Consequently few Greeks have a drinking problem.

In recent years, whisky has become almost the national drink in Greece. Even in the smallest villages far from the metropolis, the fiery local spirits *rakí* or *tsikoudiá* have been relegated to second place. The Greeks drink 45 million bottles of whisky per year – which means that they are bounding up the league tables of the greatest per capita consumers of whisky in the world.

Culture

Compared to the classical one, modern Greek culture is but a short, pathetic footnote in a volume of monumental proportions. Yet, judged independently, without the burden of its classical heritage, it is far from insignificant.

Its writers and poets (two Nobel prize winners among them) have produced, and continue to produce, works that could have made quite an impact in global literary terms had they been written in a more widely spoken language. Its composers, painters and artists often gain international acclaim. In fact, more often they first become famous abroad and then receive the plaudits of their fellow countrymen.

All this, however, is beyond the average Greek. There are households where the only books (apart from school-books) ever to cross the threshold are a couple of garishly gilded encyclopaedia sets entirely for decoration. It was not so long ago when mothers would say: "I bought you a book last year, what do you need another for?"

Most Greeks read nothing heavier than newspapers and popular magazines, the more sensational, the better. The books that are enjoyed most are bestsellers or mass market paperbacks – novels, crime stories, romances, either in translation or by Greek authors. Serious work rarely sells more than a couple of thousand copies since only one Greek in four reads one book a year. The same applies to classical music, theatre and the fine arts: when something really good is produced, it is appreciated and enjoyed only by an elite. Apart from the one state-owned classical music station, classical music is only played on the radio when someone famous dies.

All in all, in modern Greece, culture and the average Greek are like two trains running on parallel lines: they seem destined never to meet. Yet in Greece, you can never tell. A current sign of interest in things cultural may mean that the lines do not run true after all.

Meaningful Music

The actual conduit by which culture flows into a Greek's veins is music. When the verses of important Greek poets, like Gatsos, Ritsos or Nobel prize winners Elytis and Sepheris, were put to popular music by composers of the calibre of Theodorakis or Hadzidakis, they were sung all over Greece. Their beautiful, elliptical verses express love and betrayal, joy and death, past glories and lost causes:

> There is only one swallow and the spring is dear,
> To make the sun turn about takes a lot of work.
> It needs thousands of dead to push at the wheels,
> It needs the living, too, to keep offering their blood.

> On the blond sand of the beach
> We wrote her name.
> Nicely the breeze blew,
> And the writing was erased.

> Don't cry for the Roman nation.
> At the point of knuckling under,
> When the knife has reached the bone
> and the yoke is at its neck,
> It jumps up anew, and takes courage and grows bold,
> And pierces the dragon with the sun's spear.

> Spiritual sun of Justice, and you glorifying myrtle,
> Do not, please, do not forget my country.

Such heroic, poignant, often melodramatic words have an instant appeal for the Greeks – of whom writer Edith Hamilton once said, 'They are never sad. They just become elegiac.'

It is natural for the extrovert Greek to express his soul through the emotional language of music – and given the right circumstances, sometimes he succeeds. The title tune of *Never on Sunday* typifies the popular form of genuine *rembética* (songs that originated in the sub-culture of the demi-monde). This music and folk music, along with modern works inspired by them, express the essence of what it is to be Greek.

There is an underlying sadness and sense of loss in most of the old *rembética* that is reminiscent of certain Irish ballads. They are sung to the tingling sound of the mandolin-like *bouzouki*, and their cadences (four or five themes with endless variations) are thousands of years old – echoes of many bygone civilizations.

The Greeks quote song lyrics constantly in their speech. Even radio commentators use them to underline a point they want to make. News items, political programmes, cultural reviews, etc. are liberally interspersed with popular songs (some drawn from as far back as the 1940s).

For example, the Foreign Secretary is giving an interview on a matter of vital national importance. The song following his pronouncements counters: 'You are keeping secrets, you are hiding documents...'. Another Secretary has not done very well and is under a cloud. He will be further admonished on air with a pop song whose lyrics declare: 'You are making errors, what's wrong with you?' A Union leader is explaining the whys and wherefores of the current strike and the accompanying song urges: 'Come on! Get up! Let's take to the streets!' When news bulletins were covering the Allied invasion of Iraq in 2003 they were often followed by a belly-dancing pop song featuring the words: 'In the streets of Baghdad I saw her beautiful figure, and I went mad with desire...'

Another aspect of Greek 'meaningful music' is its predilection for history. The rhythm of big hits may range from rock and rap to waltz and *syrtaki*, but the lyrics bear no resemblance to their Western counterparts. They carry so many references to historical events or figures – from recent wars to as far back as the fall of Troy – that a foreigner needs footnotes to fully appreciate the meaning, or to understand why a particular song brings tears to the eyes of its Greek listeners. The past is so much an integral part of the everyday Greek life of the present that even if you can manage to take the Greeks out of History, you cannot take the History out of the Greeks.

The Greeks not only revel in these songs when sober, they accord them their greatest accolade – i.e., these are the songs they prefer to sing when in their cups:

Cloudy Sunday, you resemble my heart,
You are a day like the one when I lost all my joy.
(it was a Sunday when the Germans entered Athens in 1941)

History, the harlot, has said that we are through...

To fight at the ramparts by day – my sword on fire –
And to hold in my arms at night a Turkish girl.
(during the War of Independence – lyrics which drew a
formal complaint from the modern Turkish government)

Mother, Smyrna is burning – our dreams are gone.
(the Smyrna Massacre in 1922)

All this sounds wonderful but there is an inevitable catch. Most Greeks believe that the louder the music the better, so the majority of live music *bouzouki* joints employ loudspeakers big enough for an Olympic stadium.

In the 'grand' night-spots with their multi-coloured floodlights, be-sequined singers and garish floor-shows, you get enough decibels to raise the dead. The Greeks call these places of entertainment *skiládica*, meaning 'dog-houses', and you can take your pick as to why, from: a) the singing is generally little better than barking, b) the atmosphere resembles the kennels of a pack of hounds in full cry; and c) if you go there often enough, you're likely to end up going to the dogs.

The cognoscenti tend to congregate in tavernas where the singers use the minimum of electronic aids or none at all and the air is thick with cigarette smoke and senti-ment. Here you can see, beautifully executed, the expressive dances of old – whether solemn or joyful, or full of oriental sensuality. One such dance is described by painter and humorist Bost:

> The man – coat unbuttoned, a cigarette hanging from his lips, bitter expression and downcast eyes – stood motionless in the middle of the floor. As if to balance himself, he opened his arms wide like wings, like a great wounded bird, and started. He was a good dancer. He belonged to another world – he didn't care about us, we didn't exist for him – he was dancing for himself only. A solemn, proud and brave man, who was at odds with God and who was challenging Death. Death was trying to grab him, the man was taking a few hesitant side-steps to avoid him. In the end the man would escape – being more cunning and daring than Death. He was positioning himself to the right, to the left, with deliberate ritualistic movements. Each step was weighted and studied as if he were avoiding land mines.'

The Greeks being the veritable nightbirds they are, all such entertainment starts about midnight and the star singers only come on stage after 1 a.m. (Police raids to enforce spasmodic Government attempts to get Greeks to bed earlier are merely regarded as a nuisance.)

No-one is bothered by the fact that the morrow is probably a working day. Happy after a night of unbridled musical passion, they will straggle tipsily to bed, and then go to the office looking like a bleary-eyed raccoon.

Language

The Greek language has changed less from the time of Plato (four centuries B.C.) to today than English from the time of Chaucer (14th century A.D.) to the present.

Greek was for many centuries the common language of the ancient world around the Mediterranean Sea. It was the language of culture and commerce; the language in which new ideas, like Christianity, were propagated. No educated Roman was without it, and thus thousands of words were incorporated into the Latin vocabulary and thence – through the scholars of the Middle Ages and the Renaissance who spoke Greek at least as fluently as Latin – passed into the European languages of today.

In the English language alone, about a third of the words are either transliterated Greek or of Greek origin. Apart from most medical, scientific and literary terms, as well as hundreds of names for plants, animals and elements, Greek-derived words in everyday use range from 'alms' to 'zoo', with thousands of surprising entries in between.

Had it not been for the Greeks who first called 'Yeshua' **Jesus**, surnaming Him **Christ** (the Anointed One), where would **Christianity** and **Christmas** be? The **Church** would have no **Bible**, **prophets**, **angels** in **Paradise**, **apostles**, **martyrs**, **bishops**, **hymns**, **carols**, **choirs**, **cloisters**, **crypts**, **monasteries**, **rosaries**, **chalices**, **parishes**, **cemeteries**, **tombs**, **idols**, **coffins**, **litanies**, **exorcists**, **heretics**, **atheists**, **blasphemers**, **satanists**, **demons**, **devils** or **dogmas** – and no-one would say **Amen**.

Nothing could be **mysterious**, **ethereal**, **tragic**, **magnetic democratic**, **nostalgic** or **automatic**. Nobody could be **patriotic**, **phlegmatic**, **animated**, **diplomatic**, **domineering**, **hilarious**, **glamorous**, **famous**, **European**, **ingenious**, **nervous**, **hysterical**, **ironic**, **gorgeous** or **anonymous**.

There would be no **strategy**, **tactics**, **politicians**, **ethics**, **aristocrats**, **butlers**, **dandies**, **nymphomaniacs**, **anarchists**, **heroes**, **history**, **schools**, **arguments**, **organizations**, **symbols**, **diamonds**, **pirates**, **treasure**, **tigers**, **roses**, **paper**, **ink**, **letters**, **boxes**, **thermos**, **cups**, **cans**, **cherries**, **diets** or **pizza** with **peppers** on **plastic plates**.

The arts would have to do without **theatres**, **ballerinas**, poets, dramatists, scenes, comedy, cinema, circuses, stars, acrobats, melodies, guitars, chords, symphonies, orchestras, television, programmes, critics, photographs and scandal.

And technology would lack ideas, architects, metal, discs, hydraulics, engines, electrics, cameras, lamps, polyurethane, varnish, chimneys, disasters, and the atom bomb.

Modern Greek may have divested itself of most of its classical trappings, yet it has retained unchanged more than 80% of its original vocabulary. The rest is made up of transliterated foreign words (Latin, French, English, Italian, Turkish and others), witnesses of the many cultural influences. For example, a Greek says party, pub, trolley, manicure, casserole, drive-in, crayon, rouge, goal, parking, toast, 'adio' and everything is O.K.

The purists complain that the young speak a kind of 'Greeklish' and that 'our beautiful language is going to pot', while the more tolerant claim that they show an inventiveness for words similar to that of Aristophanes: for example, *freakáreessa* (I am freaked out), *groovátos* (a groovy man), *crusháro* (to crush), *speedátos* (someone in a hurry).

A 'War of the Languages' has been raging for ages between the Left-wing and the Right-wing literati. The latter want the Greeks to speak 'pure' Greek (the language in which the Gospels were written, or almost), and the former want an oversimplified, colloquial form of 'demotic' Greek (that which is spoken in the street), because doing away with the past and its aristocratic language would be really 'progressive'. It is as if the British suddenly decided to drop the King's English and start teaching Cockney at their schools.

There is a middle way but it is ignored by politicians so, depending on the party in power, the Greek language goes back and forth – with the school pupils caught in the middle like the children of divorced parents.

Sense of Humour

Although many Greeks are equipped with an excellent sense of humour and razor-sharp wit, what *hoi polloi* enjoy most (and understand) is coarse farce, couched in vulgar sexual terms. 'There's no accounting for tastes,' as the Greek woman said when she was told that her son was wanted by the police.

Every season there are at least half a dozen revues playing to packed houses in which political satire (the staple of any Greek show) is interwoven with blatant sexual innuendo – often in verse, to the tune of some popular song. For example, an important politician can be described as having balls so large they plough the ground when he walks; another may be deemed so weak that he cannot get it up; and all economic measures (regardless of who is in power) are described as a cucumber up the arse of the workers.

Happily, true wit has survived the onslaught of vulgarity. Spontaneous and original humour can be found anywhere, at any time. For instance, a city had been shaken by a strong earthquake and though their houses had not been damaged many of the inhabitants took fright and chose to spend that summer night on the beach. A young man, seeing a sexy damsel all alone on a lilo, approached her with the proposal: "How about an earthquake, sweetie?" The girl looked at him through narrowed eyes and said: "That depends. How much do you rate on the Richter scale?"

Word-play and puns are so much part of everyday speech and take such unexpected twists and turns (since the Greeks will appropriate any foreign word and decline it according to Greek grammar), that colloquial language is indeed 'Greek' to anyone not bred to it.

The Greeks are very fond of jokes and always find the time to tell their friends the latest they've heard of the particular batch currently in fashion. 'Bobos', a foul-mouthed, over-sexed brat, is an all-time favourite:

> The teacher is explaining to a class the facts of life, concluding that after puberty little girls can have babies, if they are not careful. "Then I could have a baby, Ma'am?" asks nine-year-old Maria. "It would be difficult, but, yes, there have been cases –" answers the teacher. "And I?" pipes up five-year-old Helen. "You? Certainly not!" From the back of the class, Bobos' voice is heard full of confidence: "I told you, Helen, that you needn't have worried."

Custom and Tradition

In Greece everyone believes in the power of the evil eye, regardless of what he may claim to the contrary. There is not a child who does not wear a turquoise-coloured bead (sometimes with an eye painted on it), as an amulet against it – and for the same reason strings of these beads adorn the necks of horses and donkeys in the country, and rear-view mirrors in the city.

A mixture of tradition and superstition still permeates several aspects of Greek life. For example, a Greek never dares say how pretty, handsome or elegant a person looks (especially a child) without accompanying his comment with a *ptt-ptt* sound – as if politely spitting out a fragment of tobacco that has stuck to his lips. He also 'touches wood' to avert the envy of the gods whenever he is boasting of something.

It is bad luck (not to mention bad manners) for Greeks not to offer some kind of refreshment to anyone visiting their home, regardless of the hour or the brevity of the visit. Traditionally it is a spoonful of sweet preserve on a tiny plate, accompanied by a glass of fresh water, but nowadays it can be anything: coffee, pastry, chocolates, ice cream or alcohol. Custom also demands that you cannot go visiting 'empty-handed', that is to say without taking a gift, however small.

Visitors play an important role in the continuing prosperity of a home (i.e., someone who is not going to spend the night in the house is not supposed to comb his hair or cut his nails on the premises) and none more so than the person who first sets foot in a house on January 1st. Well-meaning people are therefore much sought after as early-morning visitors. They must put their right foot forward entering the house, simultaneously wishing the household 'Happy New Year'. In olden days they would bring a pomegranate, which they would hurl on the floor upon entering, the spilling of its many seeds supposedly bringing prosperity for the rest of the year.

Most customs are related to religious rituals or particular feast days, although many of them are of pagan origin and have been whitewashed with a dose of Christianity. As a rule the Greeks are not terribly religious, at least not in a bigoted, self-righteous way, because the Greek Orthodox Church does not chase after them with threats of fire and brimstone if they don't show up at Mass, nor does it poke its nose into their private lives.

A religious custom that dates from pre-Christian times is that of the votive 'offerings': people who are sick or in danger of their life vow to bring to the Saint of their choice a token of their gratitude, a sort of bribe for interceding on their behalf. It can be anything – from building a chapel to offering a candle.

The Greeks also offer a *táma*, a thin silver plaque embossed with a scaled-down model of whatever is being asked to be made healthy or saved from peril (hearts, eyes, feet, hands, children, even houses, boats and cars). These offerings festoon the frames of venerable icons, icons which are not regarded as mere paintings but as holy in themselves. A few are even purported to work miracles, and the one of the Virgin Mary in the island of

41

Tinos draws more pilgrims than Lourdes.

A charming tradition related to christening a child is that the godparent has to provide the godchild with a golden cross on a chain, plus a complete Sunday outfit, including shoes, otherwise the child will never have enough clothes on its back and will 'stumble' throughout its life.

Life After Death

The Greeks' unflagging optimism is nowhere more apparent than in their funeral customs. Since no-one considers himself a sinner, they are convinced that when they die they will go to specially reserved clouds in Heaven. Thus death does not hold much terror for them.

Funerals are very elaborate affairs, followed invariably by coffee and brandy for all who attend and by a wake (with a fish supper) for close relatives and friends. A memorial service is held on the 40th day after death, when spoonfuls of a delicious concoction of boiled wheat, nuts, seeds, raisins and sugar are eaten in memoriam.

Since cremation is against the tenets of the Orthodox Church, the Greeks rest in graves constructed of marble and surmounted by a large white marble cross. (Three years after burial the bones are dug up and placed in private cenotaphs, thus solving the problem of over-crowding.) Flowers, either fresh or plastic, and a constantly burning oil lamp in an elaborate glass case are the standard decorations. Brightly coloured plastic buckets hang incongruously behind the graves bearing witness to the regular washing of the marble slabs by devoted relatives.

Cemeteries are full of people all day and every day, and priests in vestments perambulate the avenues ready to answer the call of anyone who wishes a ten-minute memorial service sung over the grave of a relative or friend. At night, the glowing oil lamps under the tall cypresses give Greek cemeteries a serene rather than haunted atmosphere.

The belief of the Greeks in an afterlife (and a good one at that), means that Easter is their greatest religious event. It starts with Holy Week, during which nearly everybody fasts and drops into church, if only once, and for a few minutes, to hear the special Masses. This is followed by the Holy Friday procession of the flower-bedecked bier of Christ; and culminates in the Holy Saturday open air midnight Mass. Finally, fire-crackers and fireworks light the night sky to show that 'Christ is risen' and the streets fill with people bearing home their lighted candles.

Easter Day is inconceivable without lamb roasted on a spit and without cracking the shells of red-dyed hard-boiled eggs with all present at the feast. (One person holds his egg in his fist, point up, and the other hits it with the point of his egg. The latter says "Christ is risen!", the former replies "He is, truly!". Then the eggs are turned bottom up and the roles reversed.) In the end the family has a large pile of cracked eggs to peel and slice for an excellent egg salad the next day.

What Is Sold Where

Greek shops have peculiar hours which vary from day to day, from summer to winter, or even according to their wares.

The shop that is open at all hours is the kiosk: a tiny cabin, usually perched precariously at the edge of the pavement and festooned with newspapers and magazines. The vendor inside it sells cigarettes, chocolates, postage stamps, bus tickets, soft drinks to playing cards, aspirins and condoms) depending on how enterprising the owner is. If the kiosk is more up-market, i.e., if it operates from a hole in the wall, there is no end to what it may be selling.

A number of interesting combinations are offered in particular shops. For example, chemists (*farmakéon*) sell drugs, some cosmetics and orthopaedic sandals, and bakers may sell milk, yogurt and soft drinks. Bakeries will also undertake to roast on your behalf (for a fee) any dish you have ready for the oven, or to bake bread or biscuits you have prepared. They may even lend you their own huge, black baking trays for the purpose.

Since no licence is required, wines and spirits are sold at all hours from any place of business connected with foodstuffs. The only exception is election day when you can buy a bottle to drink at home but you cannot have a drink at any public place unless, of course, you can persuade the waiter to put your drink in a coffee cup.

Conversation and Gestures

A Greek cannot talk unless he has his hands free, and a soft-spoken Greek is one who can be heard only as far as across the street. Two Greeks having an amiable conversation sound as if they are ready to murder each other, and a party of exuberant Greeks having a good time could be described as a pack of hounds that has just sighted the fox. A taciturn, thoughtful-looking Greek is one nursing a bad headache.

Because they are so extrovert in character, heated discussions on every subject – politics in the lead – flare up among complete strangers in the most unlikely places. The Greeks air their views not only in the coffee houses, but in the street, in buses or in shared taxis. Such debates may last any length of time and the interlocutors may illustrate their arguments with examples drawn from their private lives (things an Englishman would not dream of disclosing even to his dearest friends), without deeming it necessary to introduce themselves. The debate over, they part as complete strangers as before.

The average Greek has definite views on everything – from space travel to the price of tomatoes. He is also fond of philosophising on life and on the nature of things, using trite aphorisms – a pastime that has won the name 'vine-philosophy', since it resembles the prattle of wine-fuddled idlers.

The Greek loves to hear himself speak, and when transported by his own rhetoric his wild exaggerations and sweeping generalisations can easily mislead the unsuspecting: there are visitors who leave Greece firmly believing that the Greeks still worship the twelve Olympian gods.

Insultingly Yours

Greeting someone from afar, either arriving or departing, you may shout "*Yia sou*" and wave, but you must take care never to wave with the fingers splayed out and the palm towards the person. This is a serious insult (equivalent to 'Damn your eyes'), usually reserved for fellow drivers who believe the road belongs to them.

When angry among strangers, the Greeks are careful not to use words and gestures that might depict them as vulgar. But, among friends, insulting gestures are quite common and are even used jokingly.

One such gesture, meaning that you couldn't care less about another person's opinion, or demand, or even threat, is to make a forceful downward and inward movement, towards one's genitals. It is usually accompanied by the phrase 'at my balls', 'at my prick' or 'at my cunt'. This means: "What you're saying is of so little interest to me that, were I to write it down, I'd use a surface that's impossible to write on."

A less common but more insulting gesture is similar to a middle finger signifying 'up yours', but the hand is turned sideways and, with a rhythmic back and forth movement, the finger pumps horizontally.

The Greeks, male and female, at all levels of society, sprinkle their speech with swear words as a matter of course – not only in anger or frustration, but also as a joke, or as a form of endearment. The expletives they use vary from common swear words to juicy sexual detail of a kind that could stun a sailor.

The most popular of all is *malákas* (masturbator) in all its derivatives, ranging from 'stupid' to 'good, honest fellow' or 'my dear friend'. The noun *malakía* generally implies 'nonsense', but also describes errors committed or things one disapproves of. *Gamó to* (fuck), like its derivatives, is used more or less like 'damn!' and, unless spoken in anger, has become more a figure of speech. When swearing in earnest though, 'fuck' is used with family or religious terms, like 'fuck your mother/father/ entire clan/God/Christ/Holy Cross/*Panaghia* (Virgin Mary)/ Holy oil lamp' and more, depending on the imagination of the speaker. (The prize perhaps should go to the old mariner who used to say "Fuck a barrel of Saints with Christ as a lid!")

Such insults being very serious indeed, if you do not want to face their full implications but simply want to swear to let off steam, you use 'my' instead of 'your' (i.e., 'fuck my mother'). This deprives the other person of the legitimate opportunity to return the compliment.

There are many other interesting flowers in the garden of Greek abusive language, e.g: 'I have a cucumber up my arse' (the work I'm doing is very difficult); 'He/she has a wide arsehole' (he/she is inordinately lucky); 'God gave him a foreskin and he's opened a tannery' (he masturbates all the time/he's a good-for-nothing); 'Take care, for I'm going to throw you into the pit with the up-yours fingers' (self-explanatory); 'He made my balls go dizzy'/'He made my balls swell up' (he's a very annoying person); 'Take your finger out of your arse' (get to work); 'He needs an up-yours finger' (he needs some pressure or some incentive in order to work); 'You've done it arse-like/cunt-like' (you've made an awful faux pas, you did a job very badly); 'I'll make him fart wool' (I'll make him tremble with fear).

'Get back in place, cunt of mine, and stop prick-sailing' denotes extreme surprise; 'Come and pull at my nipples to build up your muscles' means you're talking nonsense; and the reply to 'What shall I do with it?', is 'Roll it up and stick it up your arse' even if the object in question is a cupboard.

When calling someone names, *putána* (whore) and *pústis* (passive homosexual) are the most insulting and they are all used in combination with the above. The act – *putaniá, pustiá* – means doing someone an ill-turn or something reprehensible behind his back. *Keratás* (horn-bearing man) literally means a cuckold, but it is used regardless of its actual meaning as a milder invective.

Then there is 'donkey' or 'mule' (a boorish person); 'arse-boy' (ill-mannered, irresponsible and impudent); 'dirty dishcloth' (a worthless woman) and the expletive: *Skásse* (burst) meaning 'shut up!'.

Systems

Greek systems are a far cry from, say, the clockwork regularity of the German ones. Some work (after a fashion), some do not (usually for no apparent reason), so you need to be prepared for anything. The trouble is that even the concept of 'system' is incomprehensible to most Greeks, though they grumble all the time at the legendary malfunction of theirs.

Athens is perpetually short of water and its supply network exceedingly antiquated, with the result that in periods of drought the citizens have to cut down their water consumption or pay exorbitant fines. Drought can also cause problems to the power lines, threatening the whole country with a blackout. Too much rain and bad weather conditions pose the same threat and usually put the country in a state of emergency.

Telephones, however, have improved no end in recent years, although this deprives the Greeks of a great source of fun: accidental eavesdropping on other people's conversations, or getting the wrong number – and making new acquaintances.

Public transport appears to be innocent of any schedule, and rush hour provides proof of the old maxim: 'There is no tin in which you cannot fit an extra sardine.' The new subway of Athens is a great relief to commuters and (surprise!) it works punctually and efficiently. The also-new Athens airport is run equally efficiently and a global survey found it the cleanest in the world. But domestic flights are still not famed for their punctuality, and though the international flights run on time, the joke about Greece's national airline prompts a rueful grin:

> An aeroplane is about to land in New York and the pilot asks the control tower for the time. "If you are Pan Am," answers the operator, "the time is fourteen hundred. If you are Air France, it's two o'clock. If you are Olympic Airways, it's Tuesday."

Taxis are never available when you most need them despite the fact that Athens has more taxis than any other European capital. The situation is eased by the fact that a taxi can be hailed in the street even if occupied. As it slows down, you shout the general area of your destination to the driver. If it matches that of the other passengers, you are taken aboard, but expected to pay the full fare (from the point you got in) as if you were riding alone.

'In Greece,' so the saying goes, 'nothing is more permanent than the temporary.' However, with the intended privatisation of most public services, and the necessity to catch up with fellow members of the European Union, things are gradually improving and their function may no longer depend on temporary measures.

On the other hand, it is equally probable that in a United Europe the Greeks may be a bad influence on the other Europeans, subverting them into enjoying life more, working less, and letting tomorrow take care of itself.

One thing is certain: wherever you have an appreciable body of Greeks, very soon the particular system they are involved with will start functioning their way.

Education

There is no system the Greeks denounce more vehemently than education. As usual, no-one does anything about it – least of all the teachers. For example: formal education in the Classics has more or less been abandoned as being too onerous for the children (only a smattering is taught); spelling errors are not corrected in class lest it cause childhood 'traumas'; and most schools have a shortage of classrooms, so children are taught in shifts. (Private schools are much better, but very dear.)

Entry to universities (all state run) is subject to nationwide exams, so – since the dream of every Greek parent is to see his children graduate in no matter which field – whole fortunes are spent providing them with supplementary private tutoring. Usually the same teacher who in the morning is unable to hammer the curriculum into his students' heads, is doing it successfully in the afternoon for a whacking fee. Those who fail in the exams, and whose parents can afford it, go abroad for their studies: entry is much easier and a foreign degree carries much-coveted cachet back home.

Higher education also helps the boys postpone having to face the hardships of army life (there are various conscription terms for men, while the women's corps is made up of volunteers), but serve they will – even at the age of 35. Younger recruits call them 'grandfathers' and tease them mercilessly, but there is no way out, not unless they are prepared to plead insanity or turn up at the recruiting office in drag.

Beware of Greeks Behind a Wheel

To be a good driver in Greece, if you want to survive intact, you require nerves of steel, a trapeze artist's reflexes, and an exceptionally vigilant guardian angel.

The Greeks have a love/hate relationship with their indicators so the unsuspecting motorist has to figure out for himself whether the car in front of him is going to change lane, turn, slow down or even stop dead in its tracks without warning.

Jumping a stop sign, overtaking, and innumerable infringements of the highway code are the rule rather than the exception, as is the use of the horn at the slightest provocation. 'What is the smallest fraction of time the human mind can register?' 'The time that elapses between the moment the light turns green and the moment the Greek behind you leans on his horn.'

A driver in Greece needs excellent peripheral vision and has to look both right and left when abreast of an intersection, no matter what the roadsigns say. The rule that vehicles coming from the right take precedence over the others is invoked only after the crash, in order to establish at whose door the blame should be laid.

Motorcyclists, usually unhelmeted, slalom among the cars with blood-chilling insouciance and deliberate disregard for the fact that pavements and paved precincts are only intended for pedestrians.

Health and Hygiene

The Greeks behave like ostriches about their health: if they don't talk about their symptoms to a doctor, the ailment will go away. Nevertheless, a full description of their sufferings (down to the last gory detail) is relayed to anyone prepared to listen and, since every other Greek is a self-appointed Hippocrates, they get a multitude of diagnoses and proposed cures. In general they look at illness or health as preordained, saying: 'When your oil lamp has run out of oil, neither Saints nor doctors can be of any help.'

The populace may not like going to a doctor, but they will take medicine without a second thought, and this is why there are so many chemists in Greece – business is always booming. The majority of drugs (except for the addictive ones) are sold over the counter – and so are contraceptive pills. Thus antibiotics and other medicaments are swallowed as if they are jelly beans. Greeks never think of consulting a doctor about whether the drug that cured similar symptoms in their neighbour's third cousin will have the same beneficial effect in their case. They just take it and never look back.

When a doctor does prescribe a treatment, the Greeks seldom follow it to its conclusion. A general practitioner reports that only 50% of those in need of medical attention go to a doctor before their condition has considerably deteriorated. Of those who do, only half get their prescriptions filled, and a half of them actually take the medicine. Less than half of the last group finishes the course and goes back to the doctor for a final check-up. (Don't bother to count: it comes to about 5% of the original number.)

Hypochondriacs are rare and the only microbes the average urban Greek dreads are those that stray cats and dogs (or possibly his neighbour's pets) may be carrying. So, since the Greeks play it tough, very few believe in preventive medicine, regarding doctors as a necessary evil, i.e., they only go to them when everything else has failed.

Despite the fact that eight out of ten Greeks enjoy free medical care and they contribute only a percentage of their pay towards hospital costs or medicines, the national health system (and the more upgraded medical aid provided by various unions to their members) does not cater for their requirements. The corruption inherent in the Greek public sector is nowhere more apparent than in the majority of state-operated hospitals and in the quality of the services they provide.

Rumour has it that by slipping an envelope of money to the surgeon who is going to operate, you will ensure better-than-average treatment, not in the quality of the operation itself, which will be the same for prince or pauper, but in the little comforts and care that are required after it over which the doctor has control. Bed and ward allotment are also subject to bribes. Although nurses are real 'angels of mercy', most orderlies and attendants function rather like hotel personnel – the larger the tip (given in advance), the better the service.

A large number of state-of-the-art hospitals have been built all over Greece but many older ones still exist. These might look as if they belong to a Third World country, but behind the façade of ill-kept buildings and of not so spick-and-span wards, they boast some of the best doctors and nurses in the world.

Another factor which gives Greek hospitals their Third World look is that the relatives of the patients come and go as they please at all hours (even spending the night in the wards), not so much as visitors but as private nurses actively ensuring the well-being of their loved ones. At least four such 'visitors' per patient, per day, is the average. No wonder those who can afford it, or whose insurance or social security covers the cost, prefer the luxury of private clinics. The catch here is that their five-star accommodation and service are not always backed up by five-star doctors.

Cleanliness

The Greeks come second only to the Japanese as far as their own cleanliness is concerned. Home scrubbing is a point of honour and a favourite pastime of at least 90% of Greek housewives – hence the popular saying: 'Cleanliness constitutes one half of nobility'. Since the Greeks have little sense of privacy, all doors (bathroom excluded) are left wide open, showing that the mistress of the house is not trying to conceal any untidiness.

Greek women are inordinately houseproud. Even when they have a job, they slave away the remaining hours to keep their home clean and tidy and to cater to the needs of their families. They may have all the modern appliances, but elbow grease is what keeps the home machine running – particularly since the majority of their men, like regular Oriental pashas, expect to be waited upon hand and foot. The Greek male considers it 'unmanly' to lift so much as a little finger.

Fortunately in recent years, the best cleaning device ever invented hit the Greek home front: the Filipino girl. No-one seems to know how this started, but it caught on like wildfire and there was a time when some 500,000 Filipinos (plus others from the Far East) were working as maids in Greece – half of them illegally. Many have since returned to their homelands, having accumulated a tidy nest-egg for their dowry, but their absence has hardly been felt since the gap has been filled by Greek women from North Epirus, as well as by nationals of Albania, Bulgaria, Ukraine and Georgia who work as char ladies. So the future of the Greek housewife looks much brighter than it used to – not to mention the fact that contact with so many diverse cultures also broadens her horizons.

The care the Greeks lavish on their homes does not often extend to their surroundings. They may be seen regularly washing the pavement in front of their houses (in the cities), or whitewashing neighbouring tree-trunks (in the country), but they are notorious litterbugs and every summer mass-media campaigns admonish them to keep the countryside and the beaches clean – for shame.

Personal Hygiene

From a statistical point of view the average rate of showers per person is quite impressive. At least 50% of the Greeks shower and change clothes three times a day. The other half, however, does not deem it necessary to have even one shower a day. Hence it's best to avoid taking a bus during rush hours in summertime.

About 99% of women use one or other depilation method for legs and armpits and the market in deodorants is booming. The majority of men use only after-shave lotion, regarding deodorants as rather effeminate. Very dirty people in Greece tend to be one of three kinds:

a) old peasants, who believe that bathing more than twice a year is injurious to one's health;

b) Illegal Albanians, who have walked all the way from their country and may not have washed since the fall of the communist regime;

c) Gypsy women and children, who are in the business of convincing passers-by that they are so destitute only a 50-cent Euro coin stands between them and extinction. The women usually carry an equally bedraggled and filthy squalling baby in their arms (which they rent from its mother for a cut of the take).

Despite the garlic-flavoured dishes of Greek cuisine, garlic breath is rare. There is instead a lot of gum chewing, usually with the mouth wide open, in the best American tradition. Gum is also used as a substitute for cigarettes by those who wish to quit smoking.

The Greeks not only produce a lot of tobacco, they also smoke it – a staggering 28 billion cigarettes a year. Smoking is regarded as a proof of 'modernity' by teenagers, and given the proverbial Greek self-indulgence, it is difficult for adults to kick the habit.

Their favourite riposte to non-smokers is that of a Greek playwright at the death of a friend: 'Poor man. The doctors told him to quit smoking, drinking, gourmet food, women and late nights. And what happened? He died, miserable, but in the best of health – run over by a car.'

Crime and Punishment

Greek law is mainly based on the German Penal Code (since Otto, the first king of modern Greece, came from the royal family of Bavaria) which means that you have to prove your innocence to the court. Happily there are no strange or antiquated laws that could possibly be infringed unwittingly.

Yet, if you want a Greek to do something, you label it 'forbidden'. When the first load of potatoes was brought to Greece in the 1830s, the authorities wanted to distribute it to the famished population of Nafplion (then the seat of the government). For days there were no takers because people were suspicious of the unfamiliar tuber. Then, with a stroke of genius, the Chief of Police ordered an armed guard around the mountain of sacks filled with potatoes. Next morning there wasn't a single one left.

Greek policemen are usually very polite and helpful, unless given substantial reason not to be. Apart from chasing after ordinary criminals, controlling hooligans, and endeavouring to police demonstrations and rallies, their efforts are mainly directed towards:

a) Catching whatever members of the local Left-wing terrorist group, '17 November', escaped the major sweep the anti-terrorist squad made in 2002, when they caught (by accident) the group's hit-men.

b) Apprehending the drug smugglers who see Greece as a convenient stop-over between the poppy fields of the East and the markets of the West.

c) Preventing Greek antiquities from leaving the country in the luggage of innocent-looking tourists who claim that they picked up a few valueless pieces of marble as souvenirs. (This is an argument that cuts no ice with the police since Lord Elgin, when he carted away half the Parthenon in 1802, described his loot as 'some stones of no value of themselves'.)

d) Rounding up by the hundred the stray Albanians, Rumanians, Bulgarians, Russians and other riff-raff who cross their borders, and packing them off or imprisoning them. This is a Sisyphean* labour since they come back again and again, the border area being too mountainous to be effectively patrolled. While honest immigrants get a Green Card, work hard and send money home, these illegal immigrants prefer to join the ranks of the various national Mafias and work in league with the local talent. In the early years this influx roamed the countryside and the run-down quarters of the cities stealing anything that was not nailed down, and dealing in drugs, arms and women. The crime rate in Greece rose by 70%. However after the police force got over its initial shock, it fell hard on them, and now the crime rate is considered the lowest in Europe.

Greek prisons are not recommended either for their accommodation and facilities, or for their cooking, although foreigners residing in them are better treated than the locals. Bribes can provide comforts, but the best course is to avoid being a guest at such an establishment.

*Poor Sisyphus, who was condemned for eternity to roll a boulder up a hill but which, just as it was about to reach the top, always rolled down again.

Government and Bureaucracy

It is a well-known fact that most people get the government they deserve. Nothing could be more applicable to the Greeks. Successive governments – regardless of their political colour – have displayed the same faults as the average Greek (only more pronounced). Since nothing and no-one can make the Greeks register the fact that for the past 150 years their governments are flesh of their flesh, they complain incessantly because those they have elected to govern them fall short of their expectations.

Yet when it comes to action – that is, to forming pressure groups or banding together in any form in order to right wrongs – they shrug their shoulders and exclaim 'It's not our job', fully expecting the government to be Merlin, Mary Poppins and Croesus rolled into one. The statement 'Don't ask what your country can do for you, ask what you can do for your country' has not yet penetrated Greek consciousness to any appreciable depth.

Yet the phrase 'If I were Prime Minister...' is the favourite conclusion of a political discussion for most Greeks; and they proceed to enumerate, with great conviction, how they would solve, single-handed, all the problems that have pestered Greece for ages.

Despite their undoubted intelligence, the Greeks are a gullible people when a charismatic politician tells them what they want to hear. They follow him to ultimate bitter disenchantment, and then turn to the new charmer who steps into the limelight. They invariably expect each new leader to conjure out of thin air everything the country lacks and to offer them a new Golden Age. When he doesn't deliver, they turn nasty and vote him out of office.

In general the Greeks regard their politicians with contempt – even those they vote for. They consider them corrupt and prone to feathering their own nest. 'Who wouldn't lick his fingers if they were smeared with honey?' is the popular Greek saying, and if a politician does just this very discreetly, he incurs no blame. Dipping his whole hand in the honey pot, though, gets talked about, and provides the satirists with plenty of material for their revues, but the culprit more often than not gets away with it.

The Greeks are quick to catch the bug of fanaticism, which is fanned by the press to a degree unheard of in other countries. Civil strife has been the bane of Greek society since time immemorial. Ideals usually play a very small part in choosing sides, though you will rarely hear a Greek admit it. Adherence to a particular party depends more on whether its leader catches the public's fancy, on his powers of persuasion and on the effectiveness of his propaganda network, than on his programme or his performance. The decisive factor is always the personal benefit you may expect once the party of your choice comes to power. Whether that party will also benefit the country is a matter over which very few Greeks will lose any sleep.

Bureaucracy

Other people have bureaucracies, the Greeks have 'connections' – usually a cousin-in-law thrice removed, a *coumpáros*, or a friend of a friend – in any given ministry or public service. Everyone considers this to be only sensible in a country where one in 10 is some kind of civil servant. These friends can speed things along, sometimes as a favour, other times for a kick-back commensurate with the importance of the service requested.

However, those who do not hold a key to the bureaucratic maze find things very different. This is because bureaucracy in Greece has been elevated to a form of art: the art of making enemies of the citizens. Barricaded behind his desk, the Greek who has managed to join the ranks of the civil service becomes a 'chair-centaur' – that is, a petty dictator who is afraid of taking any decision and who delights in torturing the unfortunate citizen whom fate has thrown at his mercy.

Just obtaining a ordinary certificate – birth, marriage and so on, for the purposes of, say, getting a passport, or a licence – is a major exercise. It involves hours (or even days) dealing with at least six people, who treat you with varying degrees of indifference, rudeness and pure malice, as well as traversing miles of corridors and badly lit stairs in order to get a signature from one, a rubber stamp from another, have a tax-stamp affixed from a third, etc. Getting entangled in Greek red tape makes Kafka's *Trial* look like a pleasant walk in the park.

Yet, even without having the proper 'connections', bribing one's way through the maze usually brings results. The Greeks call it 'paying the fast-stamp tax'. Despite the authorities' attempts to put an end to this admirable sport, you have only to pose the innocent question "Can we do anything about it?" or, more boldly, "How much is the fast-stamp tax?" and if the person behind the desk is on the take, a figure will be named without blushing. If not, the question will go unanswered.

There may be civil servants who are far from slothful, who go to their office in order to work – not just to loll about reading newspapers or gossip with friends – who do their best to serve the public efficiently and courteously, without receiving 'fast-stamp' dividends, but they are an endangered species. They are calculated to be some 10–20% of the public sector's workforce and it is only thanks to them that the country has not yet fallen apart.

Business

The Greeks were the first people to have a god of commerce, Hermes (i.e., Mercury), the messenger of the gods. (He was patron god of thieves as well, but one should not draw any conclusions from that.)

Having had thousands of years of training, the Greeks are good at business – particularly when they reside abroad: on a list of the 100 richest people in the world, a surprising number are Greeks.

In general they believe in free trade, fair dealing and keeping one's word. They are quick at grasping (and inventing) complicated business and financial arrangements and they are past masters at acting as middlemen – which means that they are paid by both parties while risking nothing themselves. How do you think Greek shipping tycoons made all their money?

When abroad, Greeks conform to the business ethics of their host country. In Greece, they display all the characteristics that make a Greek admirable or infuriating: they are enterprising, industrious, and, when anything goes wrong, the epitome of improvisation; but the flip side is that they can also be lazy, indecisive, negligent, and frustratingly inefficient. There are instances when the barest minimum of personnel can achieve outstanding results in record time just by sheer willpower and ingenuity, and others which can only be described as *Parkinson's Laws* Greek-style:

Parkinson: Two persons do in half an hour the work one person does in one hour.

The Greeks: Two Greeks do in two hours the work one Greek does in one hour.

Parkinson: A person extends his work to fill the time available.

The Greeks: A Greek extends his work to fill the time available, plus half as much again as overtime.

The diplomatic manager who knows how to appeal to a Greek's better self, who has a character strong enough to command respect, who believes in fair dealing and who keeps his word to his employees will receive loyalty and unstinting effort from at least 70% of his staff.

Approximately four fifths of all businesses in Greece are family ones which ensures the loyalty of employees since most of them are connected to the owners by family ties, friendship or even regional origin. Thus the right recommendation is more important than qualifications, because the Greeks firmly believe that 'Better the known faults than the unknown merits'.

A distressing fact of Greek economic life is that the rules of the game are constantly changing. Every new government seems to feel honour-bound to change the Inland Revenue System every few years, so that only an accounting wizard can make head or tail of what applies where. Another is that the Greek IRS *a priori* mistrusts the taxpayer and resorts to Shylock-type tactics, endeavouring to collect what it thinks is its due.

Given the loopholes in the system and proverbial Greek ingenuity, the honest taxpayer who finds himself treated as a crook by the IRS while seeing those less honest than himself getting off scot-free, soon discovers a way to cheat the system. Moonlighting has become so much a national sport for the Greeks, despite the efforts of every government to suppress it, that their per capita undeclared income is estimated as equal to the declared one.

Greek society is fundamentally male-dominated, but men in executive positions are less chauvinist than elsewhere, and a less qualified male rarely rises above a better qualified female colleague on the basis of gender – provided that the latter is not only better qualified but also a fighter.

There are many women in senior positions and they encounter much less 'static' from their male subordinates and command much more respect from their male peers or superiors than they would, for example, in the United States. They succeed in their careers without having to either trade on, or forego, their femininity.

In fact, in Greece sexual harassment is not very common – even towards the traditional secretary. Since most jobs are obtained through the personal recommendations of friends or relatives, who would risk them hearing about a pass having been made at their protégée? Lures are certainly cast, but if they are not taken up, they are dropped without repercussions.

A total lack of formality prevails in most Greek businesses. Behavioural codes are minimal – and not only between equals in rank. A publisher taxed by a friend for tolerating the disrespectful behaviour of one of his printers replied disarmingly: "I've hired the man because he is a good printer, not for his good manners." This kind of informality has much deeper democratic roots than, say, the first-name conduct prevailing in most American companies, which a Greek might call mere 'window-dressing'.

Informality in manners is complemented by informality in dress which in most companies and even in the public sector is extremely casual, particularly in summer. Some kinds of dress code are loosely enforced in advertising agencies and multi-national companies, but the taboos about office wear concerning bare legs, sandals, jeans, low-cut or over-short dresses, T-shirts, etc., which apply in other countries, are almost non-existent in Greece and would only make a Greek laugh and comment: "If the company doesn't like the way I dress, it should provide me free of charge with the outfits of its choice."

On Whom Is the Joke?

A popular funny story, the catch phrase of which has become a sort of signal, meaning 'Time we got back to work!' summarises the character of the Greeks and their ability to make the best of anything:

A man dies and goes to Hell, where he discovers that Hell consists of huge cauldrons full of shit – submerged in which the sinners await Judgment Day.

Every hour they are allowed to come up for a breath of air – and then, 'Heads in!' shouts the gigantic Black overseer of the particular cauldron, hitting on the head whoever seems reluctant to resume his torment, with a preposterous wooden ladle. The cauldrons are allotted more or less by nation or country, but since the new arrival was not that bad when alive, he is given the chance to choose the company he would prefer for the rest of eternity.

He thinks hard and then suggests to the arch-Devil that the Swiss cauldron would probably be the nicest – quiet people, orderly, probably cleaner shit...

'Listen,' says the Devil. 'I like you, so I'll give you a break. Don't go to the Swiss. Their cauldron works like clockwork. You get one breath per hour, and that's that. Go to the Greeks instead.'

'But,' says the man, 'the Greeks are the most noisome, disorganised, unruly, impossible people.'

'Exactly! That's why they are better off than anyone else. Just think: their daily load of shit never arrives on time; most mornings the ladle cannot be found; the overseer either falls asleep or gets drawn into heated arguments with them and forgets to give the "Heads in!" signal. He even goes on strike every so often, demanding better working conditions. So, one way or another the Greeks get more breaths of fresh air than all the rest of the sinners combined.'

The Author

Alexandra Fiada was born and lives (as does 40% of the Greek nation) in Athens. She is unable to explain her unusually disciplined nature, but suggests an inquisitive, optimistic individualism is ample proof, if it was needed, that she is a true Greek.

A passionate lover of Greek history she became a newspaper addict at the age of five, and has read avidly all forms of the printed word ever since. Fortunately this is a great advantage in her professional life – publishing.

As editor of a number of magazines including *International History Magazine* and the Greek *Reader's Digest*, translator, and author of *A Short History of Athens*, assorted treatises, articles, scripts and documentaries, she finds work her principal pleasure. But she claims she cannot function properly without copious cups of coffee, and far too many cigarettes which she defends on the grounds that if smoking doesn't get her first, the smog of Athens will.

Meanwhile she plans for a dream house among the olive trees and a pension large enough to guarantee that her relations humour her every whim well into her dotage.